HENNY
YOUNGMAN'S
BOOK
OF JOKES

HENNY YOUNGMAN'S BOOK OF JOKES

Illustrated by
Sheila Greenwald & Fred Hausman

A Carol Paperbacks Book
Published by Carol Publishing Group

First Carol Paperbacks Edition 1992

A Carol Paperbacks Book
Published by Carol Publishing Group
Carol Paperbacks is a registered trademark of Carol Communications, Inc.

Editorial Offices: 600 Madison Avenue, New York, NY 10022
Sales & Distribution Offices: 120 Enterprise Avenue, Secaucus, NJ 07094
In Canada: Canadian Manda Group, P.O. Box 920, Station U, Toronto,
Ontario, M8Z 5P9, Canada

Queries regarding rights and permissions should be addressed to Carol
Publishing Group, 600 Madison Avenue, New York, NY 10022

Manufactured in the United States of America
ISBN 0-8216-2514-4

Carol Publishing Group books are available at special discounts
for bulk purchases, for sales promotions, fund raising, or
educational purposes. Special editions can also be created to
specifications. For details contact: Special Sales Department,
Carol Publishing Group, 120 Enterprise Ave., Secaucus, NJ 07094

10 9 8 7 6 5 4 3 2 1

To MY WIFE, whom I have abused constantly to our mutual profit.

To MY DAUGHTER MARILYN AND MY SON GARY, who had to spend many months alone while I was travelling.

To THE MEMORY OF MY FATHER

To MY MOTHER, AND MY BROTHER LESTER who travelled with me, and kept my hopes up at all times.

To MY IDOL, MILTON BERLE, who since the inception of my career as a comedian encouraged me and tried many of my jokes, and is still laughing at me.

The jokes in this book are my best. They are also the favorites of my friends in show business and in the newspaper field who have laughed and laughed when I told them. I especially owe the following a debt of gratitude for laughing the loudest:

Jackie Gleason
Bob Hope
Jan Murray
Harvey Stone
Joey Bishop
Don Tannen
Red Skelton
George Gobel
Dan Shapiro
Al Schwartz
Ed Sullivan
Walter Winchell
Leonard Lyons
Earl Wilson
Dorothy Kilgallen
Irv Kupcinet
Kate Smith
Sidney Piermont
Johnny Carson
Jack Paar
Joe Lefkowitz

Murray Kester
Joey Adams
Joe Gooter
Leo and Jean Fuld
Frank Farrell
Morey Amsterdam
Hy Goodbinder
Ted Collins
Archie Robbins
Milton Seiden
Walter Jacobs and
  family
Ida and Jack Mendes
Arthur I. Goldstein
Jimmy Kaplan
Estelle and Herman
  Davis
Hy Gardner
Jack Kalcheim
Frank Sinatra
Frankie Bradley

FOREWORD

Henny Youngman is one of the great comedians of our generation. This is not only my opinion. It's Henny's.

I've known Henny Youngman, man and joke file, for over thirty years. Unlike myself, Henny did not steal jokes from the top comedians of that era. Youngman stole from the unknowns, a word which later became synonymous with his career.

The greatest form of flattery is imitation, and one of Henny's unusual traits is that he is flattered by the fact that for many years he has been an imitation of a comedian.

Every top comedian has a special gimmick that makes him stand out above the others. Youngman's secret is in his delivery and his masterful ability to *segue* from one topic to another with such subtle-like blends as "I love California . . . Say didja hear about Mayor Wagner . . . My wife's in Miami now." Actually, Youngman hasn't got a routine, he has a master code. However, we in the business all envy Youngman's quick mind and his sharp retorts to hecklers. It was Youngman who put down a heckler many years ago with lines like "Oh, yeah?" and "Gee whiz."

I kid a lot about Henny, but actually he is one of

the fastest comedians around. He has to be, with *his* act. Henny Youngman is the only comedian who was asked to appear four times at the Court of St. James, and at each of these court appearances, he was convicted. Most comedians in the business love Henny Youngman, the same kind of love that Sybil Burton has for Liz Taylor.

I hope Henny Youngman has a lot of success.

Milton Berle

OPENING OF ALBUM

How do you like me so far?
I wasn't invited here, so I came here to see why
I wasn't invited.

I just finished filling out my income tax form. Who said you can't get wounded by a blank?

␣␣␣ ␣␣␣ ␣␣␣

A Jewish woman had two chickens as pets. One chicken got sick, so she killed the other one to make chicken soup for the sick one.

␣␣␣ ␣␣␣ ␣␣␣

A man can't find a lawyer, he picks up the Red Book, picks out a law firm—Schwartz, Schwartz, Schwartz & Schwartz. Calls up, he says, "Is Mr. Schwartz there?"

A guy says, "No, he's out playing golf."

He says, "All right, then let me talk to Mr. Schwartz."

"He's not with the firm any more, he's retired."

"Then let me talk to Mr. Schwartz."

"He's away in Detroit, won't be back for a month."

"Okay, then let me talk to Mr. Schwartz.

He says, "Speaking!"

␣␣␣ ␣␣␣ ␣␣␣

I've got a brother-in-law who's a bookie. He's gotten thirty days so many times they're naming a month after him. He's working on a new invention that will kill television—color radio.

— — —

A woman used to go to a doctor to see if she could have children. Now she goes to the landlord.

— — —

The doctor opened the window wide. He said, "Stick your tongue out the window." I said, "What for?" He said, "I'm mad at my neighbors."

— — —

My arm started to hurt me. I said, "Doctor, examine my arm." He looked at my arm, he brought out a medical book and studied it for fifteen minutes.

He said to me, "Have you ever had that pain before?"
I said, "Yes."
He said, "Well, you got it again."

— — —

I have a very fine doctor. If you can't afford the operation, he touches up the X-rays. I went up to visit the doctor with my sore foot. He said, "I'll have you walking in an hour." He did. He stole my car.

A father was explaining ethics to his son who was about to go into business: "Supposing a woman comes in and orders $100 worth of material. You wrap it up and give it to her. She pays you with a $100 bill. As she goes out the door, you realize she has given you two $100 bills. Here's where the ethics come in. Should you or shouldn't you tell your partner?"

□ □ □

John L. Lewis was down in Miami. He wore his seersucker eyebrows.

□ □ □

I went down to Miami. They told me I'd get a lovely room for seven dollars a week. My room was in Savannah, Georgia.

□ □ □

Every twenty minutes they change the rates. That's the only place you can go broke sleeping.

□ □ □

Finally got a room and bath for thirty dollars a day. I didn't go to the beach once. I just stayed in my room and watched it.

□ □ □

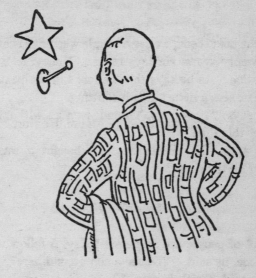

They gave me a lovely dressing room—a nail. That's the first time I ever had a dressing room where I had to tip the attendant. Everybody wants to help me carry my wallet.

To you people who are visiting: What makes you people so sure you turned off your gas back home?

=== === ===

In the next scene, we see a couple who have been married twenty years. He says to her, "Honey, let's go on a vacation." As he says this, he looks in the next room where he sees a little old lady knitting.

He says, "If you don't mind, let's go without your mother this time."

She says, "My mother. . . . I thought it was your mother all the time."

=== === ===

A lot of people are desperate today. A fellow walked up to me, he said, "You see a cop around here?" I said no. He said, "Stick 'em up!"

=== === ===

Another fellow walked up to me and said, "Stick 'em down."

I said, "You mean stick 'em up."

He said, "No wonder I haven't made any money."

=== === ===

I saw a drunk walk up to a parking meter and put in

a dime. The dial went to 60. He said, "How do you like that. I weigh an hour."

= = =

A drunk walked up to a parking meter and put in a dime. The dial went to 60. He said, "How about that. I lost 100 pounds."

= = =

Two drunks walking along Broadway in New York. One goes down into the subway by mistake. Comes up the other entrance and his friend is waiting for him.

The waiting drunk says, "Where were you?"

The other one says, "I was in some guy's basement. Has he got a set of trains!"

= = =

I saw a funny thing in Miami today. I saw a woman with a cloth coat.

= = =

There's a new perfume out which drives women crazy. It smells like money. It's called Filthy Lucre #5.

= = =

When I was a kid I had no watch. I used to tell time by my violin. I used to practice in the middle of the night and the neighbors would yell, "Fine time to practice violin, three o'clock in the morning!"

▭ ▭ ▭

What a voice I have. I'm the only one Mitch Miller begged not to sing along.

▭ ▭ ▭

I don't want to say I play fiddle bad. I'm the only one who played on "What's My Line?" and stumped the panel.

▭ ▭ ▭

Last night I ordered a whole meal in French and even the waiter was surprised. It was a Chinese restaurant.

▭ ▭ ▭

An art theatre: that's a place where the theatre is clean, the pictures are filthy.

▭ ▭ ▭

There's a new drink called Metrecal Scotch. You still

see the same things, but the elephants are skinnier.

⊟ ⊟ ⊟

They showed movies on the plane. The pilot wouldn't get on. He already saw the picture.

⊟ ⊟ ⊟

The plane was going up and down and sideways. A little old lady got nervous. She shouted, "Everybody on the plane pray."
So a man said, "I don't know how to pray."
She said, "Well, do something religious," so he started a bingo game.

⊟ ⊟ ⊟

I'm so near-sighted I can't even see my contact lenses.

⊟ ⊟ ⊟

A couple in Hollywood got divorced. Then they got remarried. The divorce didn't work out.

⊟ ⊟ ⊟

A rich guy in Dallas bought his kid a chemistry outfit —du Pont.

⊟ ⊟ ⊟

Did you hear about the rich kid from Dallas who walked up to Santa Claus and said, "Santa, what do you need?"

Want to drive somebody crazy? Send him a wire saying, "Ignore first wire."

— — —

Another way to drive a guy crazy: Send him a telegram and on top put "Page 2."

— — —

Mrs. Ponce de Leon to her husband Ponce: "You're going to Miami without me?"

— — —

You know what's embarrassing? When you look through a keyhole and you see another eye.

— — —

Want to have some fun? Walk into an antique shop and say, "What's new?"

— — —

In Hollywood they have community property. A couple gets divorced, she gets the Jaguar, he gets the little cap.

— — —

A stock broker calls up a client and says, "I think you should buy some Shapiro Uranium. It's 10¢ a share."

The client says, "Pick me up 20,000 shares at 10¢."

The next day the stock goes up to $1.00. The broker says, "You want to sell?"

The guy says, "No, get me 20,000 more shares."

The stock goes up to $3.00. "Buy me 20,000 more shares."

It goes up to $7.00. "Get me 20,000 more shares."

He says, "Sell me out at $7.00." The broker says, "To who?"

■ ■ ■

I was in the lobby of the Sherman Hotel and I found a man's hand in my pocket. I said, "What do you want?"

He said, "I want a match."

I said, "Why don't you ask for it?"

He said, "I don't talk to strangers."

■ ■ ■

My mother tells the joke about two little old ladies meeting. One says to the other, "What did you do to your hair? It looks awful—it looks like a wig."

She says. "It is a wig."

The other woman says, "You know, you could never tell."

■ ■ ■

I love Christmas. I receive a lot of wonderful presents I can't wait to exchange.

▭ ▭ ▭

A man went to Las Vegas with a $7,000 Cadillac and came home with a $75,000 bus.

▭ ▭ ▭

In Las Vegas, a man walked up to his wife and said, "Give me the money I told you not to give me."

▭ ▭ ▭

I've been married for thirty-four years and I'm still in love with the same woman. If my wife ever finds out, she'll kill me.

▭ ▭ ▭

My wife has a nice even disposition. Miserable all the time.

▭ ▭ ▭

Can she talk! She was in Miami, and when she got home, her tongue was sunburned.

▭ ▭ ▭

She missed her nap today. She slept right through it.

■ ■ ■

Valentine's Day she gave me the usual gift. She ate my heart out!

■ ■ ■

She hasn't been feeling well lately. Something she agreed with is eating her.

■ ■ ■

I said to my mother-in-law, "My house is your house." Last week she sold it.

■ ■ ■

She needed a blood transfusion. We had to give up the idea. Couldn't find a tiger.

■ ■ ■

My wife went to the beauty shop and got a mud pack. For two days she looked nice. Then the mud fell off.

■ ■ ■

My wife should have been a lawyer. Every time we have an argument and she feels she's losing, she takes it to the higher court—her mother.

She puts that cold cream on at night an inch thick, and she puts those curlers in her hair, then she puts a fishing net over the whole thing.

She said, "Kiss me."

I said, "Take me to your leader."

☐ ☐ ☐

The way she looks in the morning! She ran after the garbage man and said, "Am I too late for the garbage?" He said, "No, jump in."

☐ ☐ ☐

Now she's on a diet. Coconuts and bananas. She hasn't lost any weight, but can she climb a tree!

☐ ☐ ☐

She's tried Metrecal, safflower oil—now she eats nothing but garlic and limburger cheese. Nobody can get near her, so from a distance she looks thin.

☐ ☐ ☐

I played a horse so slow the other day, the jockey kept a diary of the trip.

☐ ☐ ☐

I have a new album out in which I play my violin. It's called "Music to Lose By."

⊟ ⊟ ⊟

Some people play a horse to win, some to place. I should have bet this horse to live.

⊟ ⊟ ⊟

The jockey hit the horse, the horse turned around and said, "What are you hitting me for? There's nobody behind us."

⊟ ⊟ ⊟

That's the first time I ever saw a horse start from a kneeling position.

⊟ ⊟ ⊟

He was so late getting home, he tiptoed into the stable.

⊟ ⊟ ⊟

I don't mind when the horse is left at the post. I don't mind when the horse comes up to me in the grandstand and asks, "Which way did they go?" But when I see the horse I bet on at the $2.00 window playing another horse in the same race. . . .

I've got a brother-in-law who's a real character. Middle-aged man, still chases women, but forgets what for.

I wish he would learn a trade so we'd know what kind of work he was out of.

□   □   □

One year he went in the breeding business. He tried to cross a rooster with a rooster. You know what he got? A very cross rooster.

□   □   □

One time he crossed a parrot with a tiger. They don't know what it is, but when it talks, everybody listens.

□   □   □

I just got him a job as a life guard in a car wash.

□   □   □

I'll tell you how to beat the gambling in Las Vegas. As soon as you get off the airplane, walk right into the propeller.

□   □   □

My mother came out there with me. Where do you think she was gambling? She was playing the stamp machine.

□   □   □

Some man lost a lot of money in Las Vegas. He's fed up, he's disgusted, he's driving out of town. From out of the mountains he hears a voice saying, "Go back to Las Vegas, go back to Las Vegas."

He figures this is a good omen, he drives back to Las Vegas at eighty miles an hour. He gets back to Las Vegas, the voice says, "Go into the Sands Hotel to gamble this time."

So he goes into the Sands Hotel. The voice says, "Play roulette, put $2,000 on Number 8." He does that. Number 6 comes up. He loses. The voice says, "How about that!"

■ ■ ■

This weather gets you nuts. One day it's cold, the next day it's nice—I don't know what to hock any more.

■ ■ ■

You know, science is wonderful. It used to take you three years to get a tuxedo shiny. Now you buy it ready-made shiny.

■ ■ ■

You know there's a new cloth you can wear in the rain. It gets wet, but you can wear it in the rain!

■ ■ ■

I bought a suit that comes from London. It was brought here and sold to a wholesaler. The wholesaler sold it to a retailer and the retailer sold it to me. To think all those people are making a living out of something I haven't paid for.

▭ ▭ ▭

Once I asked Leo Durocher to get me seats for the World Series. He said, "Leave it to me." He got me seats. From where I sat, the game was just a rumor.

▭ ▭ ▭

I was up so high I was getting spirit messages.

▭ ▭ ▭

The usher took me half way up the stairs. He said, "You'll have to go the rest of the way yourself. From here on my nose starts to bleed!"

▭ ▭ ▭

I was the only one in my row without a harp.

▭ ▭ ▭

I said to the man next to me, "How do you like the game?" He said, "What game? I'm flying the mail to Pittsburgh."

■ ■ ■

An actress in Hollywood got divorced, she took her four kids with her. There was an actor out there who got divorced, and he took his four kids with him. Then they met, they fell in love, they got married and had four kids of their own. One day she looked out the window, she said, "Darling, your kids and my kids are beating the heck out of *our* kids!"

■ ■ ■

Want to have some real laughs? Go to your neighbor's house, go into the bathroom, lock the door, run a quarter of a tub of hot water and throw in twenty boxes of jello.

■ ■ ■

A fellow walks into the Stage Delicatessen in New York and orders barley and bean soup. The Chinese waiter says, "Nemnisht," which means in Jewish, "Don't take that." The man was astounded. He walks over to Max, who owns the Stage Delicatessen and says, "Where did you get the Chinese waiter who speaks Jewish?" Max says, "Don't say anything. He's in the country four months—he thinks I'm teaching him English."

34

All you married men, want to drive your wives crazy? When you go home, don't talk in your sleep —just *grin*.

A fellow tries to cross the Mexican border on his bicycle. He's got two big bags on his shoulders. The guard says, "What's in the bags?"

He says, "Sand."

The guard says, "Get them off—we'll examine them."

The fellow takes the two bags off, they empty them out, they look through it, find nothing but sand. The guy puts the sand back in the bags, puts the bags back on his shoulders, the little fellow crosses the border on his bicycle.

Two weeks later, same thing. "What have you got there?"

"Sand."

"Get them off, we'll examine them."

They take them off, look through them and find nothing but sand. Put the sand back in the bags, back on the shoulders, he crosses the border on his bicycle.

Every two weeks for six months this goes on. Finally one week the fellow didn't show up and the guard meets him downtown.

He says, "Buddy, you had us crazy. We knew you were smuggling something. I won't say anything—what were you smuggling?"

The guy says, "Bicycles."

▭　▭　▭

A space man landed in front of Pumpernick's Delicatessen down in Miami Beach. The wheels on the airplane broke. He sees the bagels in the window. He walks in, he says, "Give me two wheels for my airplane."

The guy says, "These are bagels—you eat them."

He says, "Give me two wheels, I need them for my airplane."

The guy says, "These are bagels—you eat them—here, try one."

So the space man takes a bite of the bagel, he says, "You know, this would go good with lox."

▭ ▭ ▭

Some people ask, "What are your favorite jokes and how do you become a comedian?" Well, to become a comedian, you tell your friends a lot of jokes, you get them all together, you keep the good ones, before you know it you're a riot at a party. Somebody says, "You ought to go on the stage." Like an idiot, you believe them.

▭ ▭ ▭

Now to do this you must go to diction school. They teach you how to speak clearly. To do this they fill your mouth with marbles and you're supposed to talk clearly right through the marbles. Now every day you lose one marble. When you've lost all your marbles. . . .

▭ ▭ ▭

They've been making a lot of life stories in Hollywood. They made the life story of Jolson, they made the life story of Joe E. Lewis, they made the life story of Lillian

37

Roth. Why don't they make the story of my life? I might have lived.

▭ ▭ ▭

Here's my life story. I came from a very poor family. They couldn't afford to have children, so our neighbor had me.

▭ ▭ ▭

Things were rough when I was a baby. No talcum powder.

▭ ▭ ▭

Eleven kids in our family We were so poor we had to wear each other's clothes. It wasn't funny—I had ten sisters.

▭ ▭ ▭

My father was never home, he was always away drinking booze. He saw a sign saying "Drink Canada Dry." So he went up there.

▭ ▭ ▭

My father used to talk to me, he'd say, "Listen, Stupid,"—he always called me "Listen."

He didn't ask me to leave home, he took me down to the highway and pointed.

I met my first girl, her name was Sally. Was that a girl—was that a girl. That's what people kept asking.

━ ━ ━

Every girl has the right to be ugly, but she abused the privilege.

━ ━ ━

She had bags *over* her eyes.

━ ━ ━

She will never live to be as old as she looked.

━ ━ ━

Four drunks looked at her, they took the pledge.

━ ━ ━

It's the old story—she wanted furs, diamonds, sen-sen.

━ ━ ━

I never had a penny to my name, so l changed my name.

━ ━ ━

Uncle Sam called me. I flew my own plane for two years. Then the rubber band broke.

☐ ☐ ☐

Sally, you were so bow-legged that when you sat around the house, you really sat around the house.

☐ ☐ ☐

Your cute little nose—the way it turned up, then down, then sideways.

☐ ☐ ☐

I can't forget the way your lovely hair grew halfway down your back. Too bad it didn't grow on your head.

☐ ☐ ☐

Your left eye was so fascinating your right eye kept looking at it all the time.

☐ ☐ ☐

I used to take you riding in my car, and you insisted I take the top down. It took me three hours. It wasn't a convertible.

☐ ☐ ☐

A woman driver hit a guy and knocked him six feet in the air. Then she sued him for leaving the scene of the accident.

□ □ □

Another lady hit a guy, she yelled, "Watch out!" He said, "What—are you coming back?"

□ □ □

An Australian fag disgusted with the men in the U.S.A.: "I'm going back to my Sydney!"

□ □ □

For a young man, it's wine, women and song. For me, it's Metrecal, the same old gal and "Sing Along With Mitch."

□ □ □

I own a hundred and fifty books, but I have no bookcase. Nobody will *lend* me a bookcase.

□ □ □

Here's a recipe for a Thanksgiving turkey: Take a fifteen-pound turkey, pour one quart of Scotch over it and put it in the oven for half an hour. Take it out and pour one quart of gin over it, put it back in the oven for another half hour. Take it out and pour one quart of Burgundy wine over it, put it back in the oven for another half hour. Then you can take the turkey out of the oven and throw it out the window. But oh—what a gravy!

My mother-in-law, she's very modern. She uses L'Aimant Perfume, smells like the Coty girl, and looks like Mr. Clean.

◻ ◻ ◻

They have a new thing nowadays called Nicotine Anonymous. It's for people who want to stop smoking. When you feel a craving for a cigarette, you simply call up another member and he comes over and you get drunk together.

◻ ◻ ◻

It doesn't matter if you let money slip through your fingers, or even if you let love slip through your fingers; but if you let your fingers slip through your fingers, you're in trouble.

◻ ◻ ◻

I went up to my tailor. I finally had enough money to have a suit made to order. The suit came out awful. All disheveled. I walked down the street. A fellow walked up to me and said, "Who is your tailor?"

I said, "Why?"

He said, "Anyone who can fit a deformed figure like yours is good enough for me."

◻ ◻ ◻

When a woman puts on a dinner dress, it doesn't necessarily mean she's going to dinner. And when she dons a cocktail dress, it doesn't mean necessarily that she's going to a cocktail party. But when she puts on a wedding dress, you know she means business.

I'll never forget one day I was practicing the violin in front of a roaring fire and then my father walked in and he was furious. We didn't have a fireplace.

⊂ ⊂ ⊂

Saw some swell ads in the paper the other day. "Young man, Democrat, would like to meet young lady, Republican. Object: third party!"

⊂ ⊂ ⊂

I walked into a barber shop today and the guy nearly scared me to death. He was ordering supplies, and he ordered two bottles of hair tonic, one bottle of shaving lotion, and two dozen bottles of iodine!

⊂ ⊂ ⊂

The cutest little girl was giving me a manicure. I said, "How's about a date later?"
She said, "I'm married."
I said, "So call up your husband and tell him you're going to visit a girl friend."
She said, "Tell him yourself—he's shaving you."

⊂ ⊂ ⊂

You know, when I was a baby I cried an awful lot, but my mother said she wouldn't change me for a million.

My father said, "Maybe if you'd change him he'd stop crying."

▭ ▭ ▭

One guy came home and said to his wife, "Someone showed me an amazing device that sews buttons right on clothes."

His wife said, "That's wonderful. What is it?"

And the guy said, "A needle and thread."

▭ ▭ ▭

At the ball game today, one fellow started to bawl out the ump. Finally the ump was getting sore, so the fellow said, "I'm not really mad. This is just for the TV audience."

▭ ▭ ▭

When I was a kid I had the cutest little button nose. But they couldn't feed me. It was buttoned to my lower lip.

▭ ▭ ▭

My aunt said to her husband, "Max, last night I dreamed you bought me a fur coat." He husband said, "In your next dream, wear it in good health."

▭ ▭ ▭

Calling all cops—calling all cops—be on the look-out—they are passing a lot of counterfeit tens and twenties—be careful when accepting bribes.

■ ■ ■

You should have seen the shape on this girl. She looked like a pair of pliers wearing a band-aid.

■ ■ ■

I finally found out how they make ladies' bathing suits. First they take a stitch of nylon. That's all!

■ ■ ■

I wouldn't say her bathing suit was skimpy, but I saw more cotton on top of an aspirin bottle.

■ ■ ■

Somebody once asked me, "Henny, do you like bathing beauties?" I said, "I don't know, I never bathed any."

■ ■ ■

There's a new law that doesn't allow you to change your clothes on the beach any more. But that doesn't bother me. I change my clothes on the bus on the way down to the beach.

⊏⊐ ⊏⊐ ⊏⊐

I fell asleep on the beach and burned my stomach. You should see my pot roast!

⊏⊐ ⊏⊐ ⊏⊐

I like those chairs on the boardwalk in Atlantic City, the ones you sit in and a fellow pushes you. When I was playing there, I got in one and the fellow said, "Pardon me, but you look familiar to me."

I said, "My name's Henny Youngman, I'm appearing at the steel pier."

He said, "I saw your act!" So I got out and pushed him.

⊏⊐ ⊏⊐ ⊏⊐

Have any of you folks seen me on television? Well, my wife must be right. She can't see me either.

⊏⊐ ⊏⊐ ⊏⊐

One thing I like about the beach. There's nothing like getting up at 6:oo in the morning, putting on your bathing suit, jumping in the ocean, swimming out five or six miles, and then swimming back. There's nothing like it, so why do it?

■ ■ ■

A girl I knew came back from Miami so brown I gave her a practical birthday gift—saddle soap.

■ ■ ■

Doctors are worried about their public image these days. I don't wonder why. A few weeks ago a doctor friend of mine had trouble with his plumbing. The pipes in his bathroom began to leak. The leak became bigger and bigger. Even though it was 2:00 A.M., the doctor decided to phone his plumber. Naturally, the plumber got sore being awakened at that hour of the morning.

"For Pete's sake, Doc," he wailed, "this is some time to wake a guy."

"Well," the doctor answered testily, "you've never hesitated to call me in the middle of the night with a medical problem. Now it just happens I've got a plumbing emergency."

There was a moment's silence. Then the plumber spoke up. "Right you are, Doc," he agreed. "Tell me what's wrong."

The Doctor explained about the leak in the bathroom.

"Tell you what to do," the plumber offered. "Take two aspirins every four hours, drop them down the pipe. If the leak hasn't cleared up by morning, phone me at the office."

Fellow bought a mouse-trap for his cellar. When he went to set it, he found that he had forgotten to buy cheese, so he cut a piece of cheese from a magazine and placed this in the trap. Surprisingly enough this worked. When he went down the next morning, he found in the trap—a picture of a mouse.

I know a guy who used to be a test pilot in a suspender factory. But they let him go when they found out he was round-shouldered.

▭ ▭ ▭

Before that he worked in a winery, stepping on grapes. He got fired one day when they caught him sitting down on the job.

▭ ▭ ▭

My car is so worn out, every time I have to go down to the finance company to make a payment on it, I have to take a cab.

▭ ▭ ▭

I took my car down to see what I could get for it on a trade-in. One dealer took a look at it and offered me a ball-point pen.

▭ ▭ ▭

What a car! In order to go over ten miles an hour I have to remove the license plates. The car just won't pull that kind of a load.

▭ ▭ ▭

I took a look at my tires the other day. I've seen more rubber on the end of a pencil.

▭ ▭ ▭

Those aren't dents in my fenders, those are old-age wrinkles.

▭ ▭ ▭

Have you seen the new cars yet? They have a long pole sticking out in front with a boxing glove on the end of it. That's in case the car meets a woman driver, it fights back.

▭ ▭ ▭

I got a Volkswagen with four gears. The fourth gear is for going through Jewish neighborhoods.

▭ ▭ ▭

The two biggest features on the new cars are airbrakes and unbreakable windshields. You can speed up to one hundred miles an hour and stop on a dime. Then you press a special button and a putty knife scrapes you off the windshield.

▭ ▭ ▭

But the new cars are really something. One car has a new safety device in case your wife is a back seat driver. You press a button, a trap door opens and she drops right out onto the highway.

I understand one company has a new car that tops them all. No clutch, no brake, no motor. There's only one trouble with it. They can't drive it out of the factory.

▭ ▭ ▭

And the color schemes on the new cars are terrific. One dealer offered me a choice—paint or wallpaper.

▭ ▭ ▭

This is National Gasoline Week. Be good citizens, get out on the highway and run out of gas.

▭ ▭ ▭

They've got a new batch of crazy songs nowadays. Have you heard "The Traffic Song"? U-U-U, you musn't make a U-U-U.

▭ ▭ ▭

I just solved the parking problem. I bought a parked car.

▭ ▭ ▭

Then there's a song called "Oh." It's a direct steal from a song I once wrote called "Ouch."

▭ ▭ ▭

More songs. "I'm Walking Behind You"—Please don't stop short! "I Saw Mommy Kissing Santa Claus"—in *November?* "I've Got the World on a String"—Hold tight everybody, I might let go.

━ ━ ━

Then there's the song I sing to my wife every night—"P.S. I Love You." "P.S."—Poor Sadie.

━ ━ ━

If anyone is thinking of sending me a Christmas gift this year, please don't bother. Just let me know where you live and I'll come and pick it up myself.

━ ━ ━

I feel good today—I was up at the crack of six this morning. Took a brisk walk to the bathroom and was back in bed at 6:05.

━ ━ ━

One fellow walked into the club and asked for change for twenty bucks, and they made him a partner.

━ ━ ━

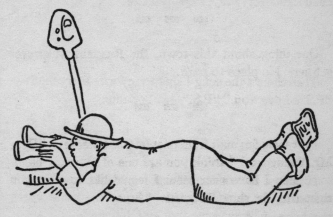

Things are rough. People are worried. I saw a man lying in the gutter, I walked up and said, "Are you sick? Can I help you?"

He said, "No, I found a parking space, I sent my wife out to buy a car."

A man called up and said, "What time does the show go on?"

"What time can you make it?" was the reply.

■ ■ ■

One thing about this town, the Russians will never get here. No place to park.

■ ■ ■

I get some fan mail from people. One letter said, "Dear Mr. Youngman: I think you are one of the most handsome men I have ever seen. I would like to meet you right after the show." Signed—"Bruce"!

■ ■ ■

Another fan letter: "Dear Mr. Youngman: I am an ex-convict. I am a fan of yours. I am about to get out of jail shortly and am about to get married to a young lady who was also in jail. She'd like to know something about my family. Well, everybody knows my father used to take narcotics, my mother sold narcotics, I have a brother who's a used car dealer, and I have another brother who is now in jail for assault and battery. Do you think I should tell her about my brother who is a used car dealer?"

■ ■ ■

My wife and I have our little fights. We had a fight last week. Nothing much—two police cars.

━ ━ ━

She puts that mud on her face before going to bed at night. I say, "Goodnight, Swamp."

━ ━ ━

My wife spends a fortune on cold creams and oils, puts them all over her body. I went to grab her, she slid out of bed.

━ ━ ━

One thing I will say, she's very neat around the house. If I drop ashes on the floor, she's right there to pick them up. I throw my clothes down, she hangs them up immediately. I got up at three the other morning, went in the kitchen to get a glass of orange juice, I came back, I found the bed made.

━ ━ ━

Walked into a store and said, "This is my wife's birthday. I'd like to buy her a beautiful fountain pen." The clerk winked at me and said, "A little surprise, huh?" I said, "Yes, she's expecting a Cadillac."

You've got to compromise when you're married. My wife wanted a fur coat, I wanted an automobile. We compromised. I bought her a fur coat, we keep it in the garage.

I bought her a mink outfit—a rifle and a trap.

She likes those little foreign cars. I bought her two—one for each foot.

If they get any smaller! I got hit by one, I had to go to the hospital and have it removed.

Three weeks ago she learned how to drive it. Last week she learned how to aim it.

I came home last night, by accident, and there's the car in the dining room.

I said to my wife, "How did you get the car in the dining room?"

She said, "It was easy. I made a left turn when I came out of the kitchen."

⊟ ⊟ ⊟

We went for a ride, she went through a red light.
I said, "didn't you see that red light?"
She said, "So what? You see one red light, you've seen them all!"

⊟ ⊟ ⊟

She put her hand out the window and signaled right, then left, then she erased it.
I said, "What kind of signal is that?"
She said, "I wanted to go right, then I wanted to go left, then I changed my mind—I rubbed it out."

⊟ ⊟ ⊟

One day she drove up the side of a building and there was another woman driver coming down.

⊟ ⊟ ⊟

Speaking of taxes—somebody somewhere must be speaking of taxes. Not me. Who's got any money left?

⊟ ⊟ ⊟

Another guy asked me for a dime for a cup of coffee.

I said, "Coffee's only a nickel."

He said, "Won't you join me?"

A panhandler said to me, "Mister, I haven't tasted food for a week."

I said, "Don't worry, it still tastes the same."

You give these fellows money, what do they do? They gamble. I can lose my own money—and I do!

I love this town. I have a lovely hotel room and bath. A little inconvenient though. They're in two different buildings!

You can imagine how big my room is, though. I close the door and the door knob gets in bed with me. And I like it.

I put the key in the keyhole, I broke the window.

The room is so small, the mice are hunchbacked.

I called down to the desk. I said, "Is this room service?"

She said, "Yes."

I said, "Send up a room."

===   ===   ===

Down in Miami I worked in a place called the Deauville Hotel. Very exclusive. Room service has an unlisted number.

===   ===   ===

Some man made a lot of money in the market. He went down to Miami for the first time, fell in the pool. The life guard pulled him out, worked on him, saved his life. The man walks over to me and says, "What do you tip for a thing like that?"

===   ===   ===

Those bell hops are tip-happy. They walk around with their hands outstretched. I was in my room, I ordered a deck of playing cards, and the man made fifty-two trips.

===   ===   ===

A little kid on the plane was annoying me with the water pistol and the water in the face.

I said, "Kid, do me a favor."

He said, "What?"

I said, "Kid, go outside and play."

These kids are nuts today. I got a kid myself, ten years old. He's going to be eleven—if I let him!

He came home from school the other day, he said, "Mother, I had a fight with another kid—he called me a sissy."

She said, "What did you do?"

He said, "I hit him with my purse."

There's a new song from my latest picture which I play on the violin called "I Was a Teen-aged Chicken Plucker."

A drunk walked into court. The judge said, "My good man, you have been brought here for drinking."

The drunk said, "All right, Judge, let's get started."

A drunk walks into an elevator shaft, falls down ten flights. He's lying there bleeding. He says, "I said *up*!"

□ □ □

One fellow put a gun in my back. He said, "Stick 'em up."

I said, "Stick what up?"

He said, "Don't mix me up—this is my first job."

□ □ □

A man fell out of a tenth-story window. He's lying on the ground with a big crowd around him, a cop walks over and says, "What happened?"

The guy says, "I don't know, I just got here."

□ □ □

A little old lady walked up to a cop and said, "I was attacked—I was attacked!"

He said, "When?"

She said, "Twenty years ago."

He said, "What are telling me now for?"

She said, "I like to talk about it once in a while."

□ □ □

A woman called up the Police Department and said, "I have a sex maniac in my apartment. Pick him up in the morning."

A little old lady goes into court, she wants a divorce. The judge says, "How old are you?"

"Sixty."

"How old is your husband?"

"Sixty."

"How long you been married?"

"Forty years."

"What do you want a divorce for?"

She says, "Aah, enough is enough."

▭ ▭ ▭

Please, Mister, I have only an hour to make a jackass out of myself. You have all night.

▭ ▭ ▭

Some people bring happiness wherever they go. You bring happiness *whenever* you go.

▭ ▭ ▭

If you had your life to live over again, don't do it.

▭ ▭ ▭

If I'm not in bed by eleven at night, I go home.

▭ ▭ ▭

An elderly man was visiting his doctor for a check-up. The doctor said, "Mr. Jones, you're sound as a dollar. You'll live to be eighty."

"But I am eighty," Mr. Jones says.

"See, what did I tell you?"

▭ ▭ ▭

Know what I got for Father's Day? The bills from Mother's Day.

◻ ◻ ◻

A woman went to her psychiatrist and said, "Doctor, I want to talk to you about my husband. He thinks he's a refrigerator."

"That's not so bad," said the doctor. "It's a rather harmless complex."

"Well, maybe," replied the lady, "but he sleeps with his mouth open and the light keeps me awake."

◻ ◻ ◻

You know something about my wife? It takes her forty minutes to get her lipstick on. Why? Because she has a big mouth, that's why.

◻ ◻ ◻

My son was annoying me the other morning, so I said, "Why don't you go out and play in the traffic?"

◻ ◻ ◻

If you must drink while you're driving home, be sure the radio in the car is turned up loud. That way you won't hear the crash.

◻ ◻ ◻

I always try to buy a little something for my wife, but I can never remember her measurements. However, I always find a salesgirl who is built like her. The other day I couldn't find a salesgirl built like my wife. One was taller. One was shorter. But a customer standing nearby was built exactly like my wife, so I said, "Excuse me, sir, what size are you?"

The other day I was offered a TV series. They want me to star in something called "The Rock and Roll Robin Hood." I dress in a black leather jacket. I ride around on a motorcycle. I carry a gun. The whole premise is that I steal from the rich . . . but I keep it.

□ □ □

The other day I went down to the Internal Revenue Department. Thank heavens! I'm all paid up until 1947.

□ □ □

Two kangaroos were talking to each other, and one said, "Gee, I hope it doesn't rain today. I just hate it when the children play inside."

□ □ □

A rugged Texan, dripping with oil and Cadillacs, walked into an exclusive art gallery in New York with his nagging wife. In fifteen minutes flat the Texan bought six Picassos, three Renoirs, ten Cézannes, and thirty Utrillos. He then turned to his wife and with a sigh of relief said. "There, honey chile, that takes care of the Christmas cards. Now let's get started on the serious shopping."

□ □ □

During a flight from New York to Los Angeles, a passenger who had been gazing out the window suddenly spied two engines on fire. He began shouting at the top of his lungs, "Two engines are on fire! Two engines are on fire!"

In a few short seconds panic and hysteria spread to the rest of the passengers. The pilot, equipped with a parachute, soon appeared in the passenger compartment. "Don't worry," he assured them, "I'm going for help."

I still love the oldie about the convict who was going to the electric chair and called his lawyer for some last advice. The barrister replied, "Don't sit down!"

━ ━ ━

There was a mix-up at the swank Fifth Avenue florist shop. Wrong cards were attached to two imposing floral wreaths. The one that went to a druggist moving to a new building read: "Deepest sympathy." The one intended for the funeral of a leading banker read: "Good luck in your new location."

━ ━ ━

Las Vegas is the only town in the country where you can have a wonderful time without enjoying yourself.

━ ━ ━

A man doesn't know what real happiness is until he's married. Then it's too late.

━ ━ ━

Show me a man with very little money, and I'll show you a bum.

━ ━ ━

I miss my wife's cooking—as often as I can.

⊟ ⊟ ⊟

One time I came home and my wife was crying because the dog had eaten a pie she made for me.

"Don't cry," I told her, "I'll buy you another dog."

⊟ ⊟ ⊟

I learned dancing from Arthur Murray. Later I found it was more fun with a girl.

⊟ ⊟ ⊟

The other day a policeman stopped me going the wrong way on a one-way street.

"Didn't you see the arrow?"

"Arrow? Honest, Officer, I didn't even see the Indians."

⊟ ⊟ ⊟

The other day a friend of mine walked into a cigar store and said to the salesgirl, "I'd like to buy a carton of cigarettes."

The salesgirl smiled and said, "There are so many brands. Which one would you like?"

My friend thought for a moment, then mentioned a

particular brand, whereupon the following conversation took place:

"Do you want the soft pack or the crush-proof box?"

"Soft pack."

"King size or regular?"

"King size."

"Filter tip or plain?"

"Filter tip."

"Menthol or mint?"

"Menthol."

"Cash or carry?"

"Forget it. I've broken the habit."

▭ ▭ ▭

Martha Raye kissed me. I lost my head completely.

▭ ▭ ▭

I don't have to do this for a living. I can always starve to death.

▭ ▭ ▭

My wife doesn't want to take weight off. She just wants to rearrange it.

▭ ▭ ▭

My best friend ran away with my wife, and let me tell you, I miss him.

━ ━ ━

My wife talks so much I get hoarse just listening to her.

━ ━ ━

The garage charged me twenty-five dollars for towing my car for a mile. I got my money's worth, though. I kept my brakes on.

━ ━ ━

I sent my income tax form in last week and didn't sign it. If they want me to guess how much I'll make, let them guess who sent it in.

━ ━ ━

Miami's so empty the life guards are saving each other.

━ ━ ━

What good is happiness? It can't buy you money.

━ ━ ━

I saved a girl from being attacked last night. I controlled myself.

◻ ◻ ◻

There's a new safety device on cars now. If you want to turn right, press a button and a sign lights up that says, "I'm turning right." Press another button and it says, "I'm turning left." There's a special button for women drivers. It says, "I don't know what I'm going to do next."

◻ ◻ ◻

My wife is learning how to drive. When the road turns when she does, it's a coincidence.

◻ ◻ ◻

"All right, Charlie, I want you to walk inside the bank, anyone gets in your way, shoot him down. Grab all the money, come walking outside. I'll be sitting in the getaway car. And remember one thing. I'll be taking all the chances."

"You mean to tell me you want me to walk inside the bank, anyone gets in my way, shoot him down, grab all the money, come walking outside. You'll be sitting in the car waiting for me and you say you'll be taking all the chances? What chances are you taking?"

"I can't drive."

◻ ◻ ◻

I never drink coffee during the day. It keeps me awake.

⊟ ⊟ ⊟

I'm not overweight. I'm just six inches too short.

⊟ ⊟ ⊟

I just found out why those guys ride bicycles up in the air on the tight wire. No traffic.

⊟ ⊟ ⊟

"Young man, you have been brought in here for driving eighty miles an hour. What have you got to say for yourself?"

"Judge, I wasn't going eighty, I wasn't going sixty, I wasn't going forty or thirty or twenty or ten."

"Give him a ticket for backing into someone."

⊟ ⊟ ⊟

I watched a new car roll off the assembly line. It's amazing. They start out with little pieces, then it rolls down the assembly line and thousands of men and a million dollars' worth of machinery put everything together. Finally a shiny new car emerges. Then a woman buys it and turns it into little pieces again.

⊟ ⊟ ⊟

Two drunks were standing in front of the Washington monument. One of them started a fire at the base of it. The other said, "You'll never get it off the ground."

The darnedest things are happening in California. I just got back yesterday. I was in Beverly Hills and never saw so many foreign cars. Milton Berle was driving an American car. The people were yelling at him, "Yankee, go home."

— — —

When I was in Hollywood I watched them make the movie *Walk on the Wild Side*. It's about a guy who tries to get on the other side of the Hollywood Freeway.

— — —

Martha Raye's been married six times now. She's got a wash-and-wear bridal gown.

— — —

The trouble with my wife is that she goes for any new vogue that comes along. She saw a picture with Jacqueline Kennedy with the hemline above the knees, so she ran right out and had all her dresses shortened. The only difference is, my wife has knees like Peter Lawford's.

— — —

They're adding a new traffic light to the standard group of red, amber, and green. If you have an accident, this one squirts iodine.

— — —

A new model has the license plates on the bottom of the car. If a guy knocks you down, you can look up and see who hit you.

◻ ◻ ◻

My wife changes her hair so many times she has sort of a convertible top.

◻ ◻ ◻

They're remodeling St. Patrick's Cathedral. They're putting in drive-in confessionals. It's called "Toot and Tell."

◻ ◻ ◻

He can't seem to find a job in his trade. He's a fog light operator in the steam room of a Turkish bath.

◻ ◻ ◻

A guy is sending a wire to his partner. He tells the Western Union operator to say, "Don't come back. Business is bad, I just laid off twenty people, the bill collectors are after me." Then he says, "And don't read it back, operator. It's breaking my heart—I can't stand it."

◻ ◻ ◻

Sam and Al had been partners for many years and they shared and shared alike in almost everything, including the affection of their pliable and rather hot-blooded secretary. One morning Sam came into Al's office extremely upset. "Al," he moaned, "something terrible has happened. Our secretary is going to have a baby. We are going to be a father." But Al, who was the calmer of the two, sat his partner down and pointed out that a great many worse things could have happened to them: Business could have fallen off, for instance. They agreed that the only thing to do was share and share alike, as they always had. They would see that their secretary got the very best in medical care, they decided, and after the child was born, he would want for nothing. A room of his own, fine clothes and the best of schooling; they would set up a trust fund after his birth to guarantee him a college education. The lucky youngster would have two fathers instead of just one. And before they knew it, the big day had arrived. The two of them paced back and forth in the hospital waiting room until Sam could stand it no longer. "I'm too nervous up here," he said. "I'm going to go down and sit in the car. As soon as something happens, you come down and tell me." Al agreed, and in less than an hour he was down on the street wearing a grave expression. It was obvious to Sam, even before his partner spoke, that something was wrong. "What's the matter?" Sam asked, starting to choke up. "Is it bad news?" His partner nodded. "We had twins," Al said, "and mine died."

▭ ▭ ▭

The place was so crowded you couldn't breathe in and out. You had to breathe up and down.

◻ ◻ ◻

One new car is so modern you press a button and *it* presses a button.

◻ ◻ ◻

My kid is a born doctor. That kid can't write anything anybody can read.

◻ ◻ ◻

Some men sleep in pajama bottoms, some in pajama tops. I just sleep in the string.

◻ ◻ ◻

Everybody's on strike nowadays. We saw a guy carrying a sign with nothing on it.

"Who are you picketing against?" I asked.

He says, "Nobody. I'm looking for a sponsor."

◻ ◻ ◻

The income tax people are very nice. They're letting me keep my own mother.

■ ■ ■

Time is so short on some of the TV programs. Just imagine yourself listening to a musical program with announcements and jokes at the same time.

■ ■ ■

My brother-in-law has an allergy. He's allergic to work.

■ ■ ■

A guy picks up a girl in a bar. She notices his cuff links and tie clasp have the insignia of a whip on them. He invites her for a ride in his Cadillac, and she notices on the door is the whip insignia, and even on the hub caps. On the cigarette lighter there's the whip insignia. They go to his apartment and there's the whip motif again on the chairs, on the bar, everywhere. He says, "I'm going to change into something more comfortable," and disappears into the bedroom. She notices a picture on the wall of a half-naked man with a whip in his hand, beating a woman. He comes back into the room wearing a smoking jacket with a whip insignia on it and says to her, "Now I'm going to make love to you."

She says, "Thank God."

We got a new foreign car with the motor in the back. Pulled up in front of the Sherman Hotel and the bellboy opened up the back of the car. Before I knew it, the motor was up in the room.

▭ ▭ ▭

The meanest thing you can do to a woman is to lock her in a room with a thousand hats and no mirror.

▭ ▭ ▭

Christine Jorgenson's mother is doing a book—*My Son, the Daughter.*

▭ ▭ ▭

A fellow is standing in a bar and another guy walks up to him and says, "Are you Joe Smith?"

The fellow says, "Yes, I'm Joe Smith."

He says, "Were you in Chicago a few weeks ago?"

The fellow says, "Just a minute," and takes a little notebook out of his pocket and riffles through the pages, goes down the line, and says, "Yeah, I was in Chicago a few weeks ago."

"Did you stay at the Sherman House?"

The guy looks through his little notebook again and says, "Yes, I stayed at the Sherman House."

"Were you in Room 213?"

The fellow scans the pages of his notebook again and says, "Yes, I was in Room 213."

The guy says, "Did you know a Mrs. Wentworth who stayed in Room 214?"

The guy looks in his book again and says, "Yes, I knew a Mrs. Wentworth who stayed in 214."

The guy says, "Tell me, did you have an affair with Mrs. Wentworth?"

The fellow scans his notebook again and says, "Yes, I had an affair with Mrs. Wentworth."

The guy says, "Well, I'm Mr. Wentworth, and I don't like it."

Again the fellow looks into his notebook and says, "You know, you're right. I didn't like it either."

▭ ▭ ▭

One beauty shop makes your hair curly for only 49¢. They stick your finger in the light socket.

▭ ▭ ▭

The traffic was so heavy people were driving bumper to bumper. I pushed in my cigarette lighter and the woman in the car in front of me said, "Ouch!"

▭ ▭ ▭

President Kennedy met my wife. He declared my home a disaster area.

▭ ▭ ▭

To give you an idea how difficult my wife can be, she bought me two ties for my birthday. To please her I wore one. She hollered, "What's the matter, don't you like the other one?"

▭ ▭ ▭

Saw something funny in the paper today. "Father of 14 Shot—Mistaken for Rabbit."

▭ ▭ ▭

He said, "I love you terribly." She said, "You certainly do."

▭ ▭ ▭

I know a guy that was so active that five years after he died, his self-winding watch was still running.

▭ ▭ ▭

The automobile of tomorrow will be faster than sound. You'll be in the hospital before you start the motor.

▭ ▭ ▭

Now that I've learned to make the most of life, most of it is gone.

▭ ▭ ▭

My wife keeps imitating Teddy Roosevelt. She runs from store to store yelling, "Charge!"

Paying alimony is like having the TV set on after you've fallen asleep.

= = =

My wife used to be a guitar player. She got rid of the guitar and now just picks on me.

= = =

A fellow walked up to me today and asked for a nickel for a cup of coffee. I gave it to him, and then followed him to the restaurant.

= = =

The first part of our marriage was very happy. But then on the way back from the ceremony. . . .

= = =

A guy buys all kinds of scuba diving equipment—$2,000 worth. He goes 150 feet down in the water, sees all the strange fish and scenery, and says to himself, "This is really worth $2,000—I'm really enjoying it." He goes down another 50 feet, sees more beautiful fish and scenery, and all of a sudden coming toward him is a fellow in just plain swimming trunks. He takes out his underwater pad and pencil and writes a note to the guy in the trunks saying, "I just spent $2,000 on all this scuba equipment and here you are all the way down in just a pair of swimming trunks. What's the idea?"

He hands the pad and pencil to the man, who writes back, "You idiot—I'm drowning."

— — —

Things are rough with me. Just got a letter from my bank. It says, "This is the last time we will spend 5¢ to let you know you have 4¢.

— — —

Americans are getting stronger. Twenty years ago it took two people to carry ten dollars' worth of groceries. Today a five-year-old does it.

— — —

The other day I was driving under the influence of my wife. She talks and talks and talks. She gets two thousand words to the gallon.

— — —

I gave my wife a car. She loves it so she's taking it to England. She wants to see what it's like to drive on the left side of the street—legally.

— — —

When I was a kid, I practiced. The neighbors threw stones through the window. Imagine being that anxious to hear me play! I was flattered.

— — —

I've got a sixteen-year-old son who is 6'3" until he gets a haircut. Then he's 5'8".

— — —

Drunk to traffic cop: "But nobody in the car was driving, Officer. We were all in the back seat."

— — —

I have a great house. It's just twenty minutes from the city—by phone.

— — —

Statistics show that every four seconds a woman gives birth to a baby. Our problem is to find this woman and stop her.

— — —

Have you tried vodka and carrot juice? You get drunk just as fast, but your eyesight gets better.

— — —

A guy goes to a psychiatrist and says, "I keep dreaming that Liz Taylor wants to take me in her arms and I keep pushing her away."

The doctor says, "My advice to you is, break your arms off."

◁▷ ◁▷ ◁▷

A guy comes up in divorce court about alimony payments. The judge says, "The Court shall grant this woman twenty-five dollars a week."

The guy says, "That's very nice of you, Judge. I'll pitch in a few dollars myself."

◁▷ ◁▷ ◁▷

Three scientists were given six months to live and told they could have anything they wanted. The first scientist was a Frenchman. He wanted a beautiful villa on the Riviera and a gorgeous woman. The second doctor was an Englishman. He wanted to have tea with the Queen. The third doctor was a Jewish doctor. He wanted the opinion of another doctor.

◁▷ ◁▷ ◁▷

Business was so bad the other night the orchestra was playing "Tea for One."

◁▷ ◁▷ ◁▷

It was so bad the cigarette girl was selling loose cigarettes.

Whisky certainly improves with age. The older my brother-in-law gets, the better he likes it.

◻ ◻ ◻

I live so far out of town in the suburbs, the mailman mails me my letters.

◻ ◻ ◻

Did you ever see one of those Italian movies, "Bread, Love and Pizza," or "Bread, Love and Mozarella"? What are all the lovers over there, bakers?

◻ ◻ ◻

They're making a new picture with Brigitte Bardot. She's fully dressed and the camera men are naked.

◻ ◻ ◻

Lately my wife's been falling in love with television heroes. When she gets a sore throat, she refuses to go to a doctor. She sits in front of the TV set with her mouth open, showing her tonsils to Ben Casey.

◻ ◻ ◻

Do you know what it means to come home at night to a woman who'll give you a little love, a little affection, a little tenderness? It means you're in the wrong house, that's what it means.

□ □ □

He's the kind of a guy who drinks Brazilian coffee out of an English cup while devouring French pastry while sitting on his Danish furniture after coming home in his German car from seeing an Italian movie, then blows his top, picks up his Japanese-made ball-point and writes to his Congressman, demanding that they stop the flow of gold out of this country.

□ □ □

It's easy to grin when your ship comes in
And life is a happy lot,
But the guy worthwhile is the guy who can smile
When his shirt creeps up in a knot.

□ □ □

A man seventy-five years old is reading in his hotel room when he hears a knock on the door and a beautiful girl says, "I'm sorry, I must be in the wrong room."

He says, "You got the right room, but you're forty years too late."

□ □ □

All you people in from out of town—what makes you so sure you turned off your TV sets back home?

☐ ☐ ☐

Two guys who work in the garment industry are hunting game in Africa. They hear the growl of an animal behind them.

One says, "What kind of an animal is that?"

The other says "What am I—a furrier?"

☐ ☐ ☐

A guy in the garment industry has a son who asks him, "Daddy, what kind of a flower is that?"

He says, "What am I, a milliner?"

☐ ☐ ☐

Two guys in the industry were having lunch together. One guy says, "Oye."

The other one says, "You're telling me!"

☐ ☐ ☐

I don't know what to get my wife any more. First she wanted a mink, I got her a mink. Then she wanted a silver fox, I got her a silver fox. It was ridiculous. The house was full of animals.

☐ ☐ ☐

A guy comes home and finds his wife relaxing in bed. All looks well till he notices a cigar in the ash tray. He becomes furious and yells, "Where did that cigar come from?"

A voice from under the bed says, "Havana!"

▭ ▭ ▭

One day in school young Johnny wrote on the blackboard, "Johnny is a passionate devil." The teacher reprimanded him for this act, and made him stay after school for one hour.

When he finally left the school that evening, all his friends crowded around him, eager to hear what punishment he had received. "What did she do to you?" asked one little tyke.

"I ain't saying nothing," Johnny replied, "except that it pays to advertise."

▭ ▭ ▭

A middle-aged friend of ours says he can't understand all the excitement over the movie version of *Lolita*. "I didn't see anything in it that could be considered even vaguely sensational," he told us, "and neither did my twelve-year-old wife."

▭ ▭ ▭

The convertible glided silently to a stop on a lonely country road.

"Out of gas," he said, with a sly smile.

"Yes, I thought you might be," said his date, as she opened her purse and pulled out a small hip flask.

"Say, you *are* a swinger," he said. "What do you have in there—Scotch or Bourbon?"

"Gasoline," she replied.

"My wife is always asking for money," complained a friend of ours. "Last week she wanted $200. The day before yesterday she asked me for $125. This morning she wanted $150."

"That's crazy," we said. "What does she do with it all?"

"I don't know," said our friend, "I never give her any."

■ ■ ■

The unabashed dictionary defines adolescence as the age between puberty and adultery.

■ ■ ■

Noah Webster's wife, returning from a long trip, discovered the lexicographer "in flagrante delicto" with a pretty chambermaid. "Mr. Webster!" she gasped, "I am surprised!"

"No, my dear," said Webster with a reproving smile. "You are shocked; I am surprised."

■ ■ ■

Hoping to avoid the embarrassing attentions that most hotels bestow on newlyweds, the honeymooners carefully removed the rice from their hair, took the "Just Married" sign off their car, and even scuffed their luggage to give it that traveled look. Then, without betraying a trace of their eagerness, they ambled casually into Miami

Beach's Fontainebleau Hotel and up to the front desk, where the groom said in a loud, booming voice, "We'd like a double bed with a room."

The unabashed dictionary defines incest as sibling revelry or a sport the whole family can enjoy.

Many a girl succeeds in keeping the wolf from her door these days by inviting him in.

In her own eyes, Peggy was the most popular girl in the world. "You know," she said, with characteristic modesty, "A lot of men are going to be miserable when I marry."

"Really?" said her date, stifling a yawn. "How many are you going to marry?"

We just got the word about the legal secretary who told her amorous boy friend, "Stop and/or I'll slap your face."

Sugar daddy: A man who can afford to raise Cain.

▭ ▭ ▭

A gravedigger, thoroughly absorbed in his work, dug a pit so deep one afternoon that he couldn't climb out when he had finished. Come nightfall and evening's chill, his predicament became more uncomfortable. He shouted for help and at last attracted the attention of a drunk staggering by.

"Get me out of here," the digger pleaded. "I'm cold!"

The inebriated one peered into the open grave and finally spotted the shivering digger in the darkness.

"Well, no wonder you're cold, buddy," said the drunk, kicking some of the loose sod into the hole. "You haven't got any dirt on you."

▭ ▭ ▭

We know a girl who thinks she's a robot just because she was made by a scientist.

▭ ▭ ▭

A man is old when his dreams about girls are re-runs.

▭ ▭ ▭

Alimony: Bounty on the Mutiny.

▭ ▭ ▭

The psychiatrist leaned back and placed the tips of his fingers together while he soothed the deeply troubled man who stood before him. "Calm yourself, my good fellow," he gently urged. "I have helped a great many others with fixations far more serious than yours. Now let me see if I understand the problem correctly. You indicate that in moments of great emotional stress, you believe that you are a dog. A fox terrier, is that not so?"

"Yes, sir," mumbled the patient. "A small fox terrier with black and brown spots. Oh, please tell me you can help me, doctor. If this keeps up much longer, I don't know what I'll do."

The doctor gestured toward his couch. "Now, now," he soothed, "the first thing to do is lie down here and we'll see if we can't get to the root of your delusion."

"Oh, I couldn't do that, Doctor," said the patient. "I'm not allowed up on the furniture."

━ ━ ━

A manager brings a dog into a night club to work. The dog is a brilliant piano player—plays Bach, Beethoven, everything. He's sitting there playing and all of a sudden a big bushy-haired dog comes in and pulls him off the stool. The owner of the club says to the dog's manager, "What happened?"

He says, "Ah, they want him to be a doctor."

━ ━ ━

Nieman Marcus in Dallas is very good to their customers. A woman broke her leg, they had it gift wrapped.

I want to send my brother-in-law a gift for Christmas. What do you give a guy who's had everybody?

□ □ □

Taxes are still going up. Somebody has to pay for Caroline's piano lessons.

□ □ □

It was so crowded at Macy's, I rested my elbow on the counter and somebody sold it for $1.98.

□ □ □

I will never forget my school days. I was teacher's pet. She couldn't afford a dog.

□ □ □

There's nothing wrong with my wife that a miracle won't cure.

□ □ □

My wife eats so fast she makes sparks come out of her knife and fork.

□ □ □

I went to a very swanky party the other day. They didn't serve napkins, the waiters walked around with roller towels.

A bunch of ten guys had a very poor friend, a real hard-luck guy they wanted to help out. They decided to have a raffle and let him win, so they made all the tickets number 4 except his. They put all the tickets in a hat and let him draw. He sticks his hand in the hat and pulls out 6⅞.

= = =

A friend of mine was complaining that the new house he rented had grass growing through the living room floor.

I asked, "How much rent are you paying?"

He said, "Forty dollars a month."

I said, "What do you expect for forty dollars a month —broccoli?"

= = =

I used to be a fighter. They used to call me Canvasback Youngman.

= = =

I used to go into the ring vertical and come out horizontal.

= = =

I had so much resin on my back that whenever I passed Carnegie Hall the fiddles used to stand at attention.

〓 〓 〓

I was the first guy to fight a four-way cold tablet six ways.

〓 〓 〓

I did pretty good at the beginning, I won my first ten fights, then I ran into trouble. They made me fight a man.

〓 〓 〓

What a fight! When the bell rang, I came out of my corner and threw six straight punches in a row. Then the other guy came out of his corner.

〓 〓 〓

First he threw a right cross, then he threw a left cross. Then came the Red Cross.

〓 〓 〓

He came up to about my chin. The trouble was he came up too often.

■ ■ ■

My best punch was a rabbit punch, but they would never let me fight rabbits.

■ ■ ■

In the fifth round I had my opponent worried. He thought he killed me. But in the sixth round I had him covered with blood—mine!

■ ■ ■

My favorite sport now is baseball. I went to the game today. It seems everybody went to the game today. The subways were so crowded even the men were standing.

■ ■ ■

But I'm always a gentleman in the subway. Whenever I see an empty seat I point it out to a lady, then I race her for it.

■ ■ ■

A terrible thing happened to me on the subway. The paper I was reading got off at Ninety-sixth Street.

You meet the craziest people on the subway. One guy sitting next to me kept saying, "Call me a doctor—call me a doctor."

I asked, "What's the matter, are you sick?"

He said, "No, I just graduated from medical school."

▭ ▭ ▭

Another guy kept running around the train yelling, "I'm George Washington—I'm George Washington." The conductor yelled, "Valley Forge," and the guy got off.

▭ ▭ ▭

I just bought a little Italian car. It's called a Mafia. There's a hood under the hood.

▭ ▭ ▭

Jack the Ripper was never killed. I think he's doing my shirts.

▭ ▭ ▭

Income tax: That's the government's version of instant poverty.

▭ ▭ ▭

A little boy never said a word for six years. One day his parents served him cocoa. From out of left field the kid says, "This cocoa's no good."

His parents went around raving. They said to him, "Why did you wait so long to talk?" He said, "Up till now everything's been okay."

— — —

We got a new garbage disposal—my brother-in-law. He'll eat anything.

— — —

There's a new kind of push-button car. In case you get stuck in heavy traffic, you push a button, you get out and take a cab.

— — —

Want to get a bootblack crazy? Next time you go in for a shine, wear one black shoe and one brown shoe.

— — —

A guy walks into psychiatrist's office and says, "Doc, I'm going crazy. I keep imagining I'm a zebra. Every time I look at myself in the mirror my entire body seems covered with black stripes."

The doctor says, "Now calm down, go home and take these pills, get a good night's sleep and I'm sure the black stripes will disappear." The guy goes home, takes the pills, and comes back two days later. He says, "Doc, I feel great. Got anything for the *white* stripes?"

◻ ◻ ◻

Have you noticed the album covers lately? Beautiful pictures of gorgeous, well-built girls. You open it up and what've you got? A flat record!

◻ ◻ ◻

Just found a labor-saving device—a rich old lady.

◻ ◻ ◻

Whistler's mother was doing a handstand. Her son asked, "What's the matter, Ma, you off your rocker?"

◻ ◻ ◻

There's a new kind of Russian roulette. You get six cobras in a room and you play a flute. One of them is deaf.

◻ ◻ ◻

My dad was the town drunk. A lot of times that's not so bad—but New York City?

◻ ◻ ◻

Did you hear about the near-sighted snake who fell in love with a piece of rope?

You see some of the craziest things in restaurants. I saw a guy put ten spoons of sugar into his coffee and then start to drink it. I said, "How come you don't stir it?"

He answered "I don't like it sweet!"

▭ ▭ ▭

When it comes to gambling, I only gamble for laughs. In fact, last week I laughed away my car.

▭ ▭ ▭

There's a new medical show. It's called Perry Casey. It's about a lawyer who owns his own ambulance.

▭ ▭ ▭

They had a fire in a hotel in Miami Beach. A woman shouted, "Help—fire—Cha-Cha-Cha!"

▭ ▭ ▭

Say, what do you send to a sick florist?

▭ ▭ ▭

ADVICE JOKES

Question: My child has a nail-biting habit. How can I stop him from biting his nails all the time?

Answer: That's easy, lady. Just have his teeth yanked out.

▭ ▭ ▭

Question: Two men are in love with me, Murray and George. Who will be the lucky one?

Answer: Murray will marry you. George will be the lucky one.

▭ ▭ ▭

Question: I've been married for five years and my husband still keeps his old address book. Is that fair?

Answer: Of course that's fair. When you buy a new car you always carry a spare, don't you?

▭ ▭ ▭

Question: I like to read a book and am constantly annoyed by my small son sliding down the banister. How can I stop him from sliding down the banister?

Answer: Put some barbed wire on the banister. That won't stop him, but it will certainly slow him down.

▭ ▭ ▭

Question: I came home late one night and my wife began hitting me with a baseball bat. When she got tired, her six brothers and her father all took turns hitting me with the bat. Is that legal?

Answer: It's perfectly legal for a woman to hit her husband with a baseball bat, but she is not allowed to bring in so many pinch hitters.

▭ ▭ ▭

My wife is the sweetest, most tolerant, most beautiful woman in the world. This is a paid political announcement.

▭ ▭ ▭

PSYCHIATRIST JOKES

I went to see a psychiatrist. He said, "Tell me everything." I did, and now he's doing my act.

▭ ▭ ▭

A mother took her little boy to a psychiatrist and asked, "Can a boy ten years old marry a beautiful star like Liz Taylor?"

The psychiatrist said, "Of course not, it's impossible."

The mother said to the kid, "See, what did I tell you. Now go and get a divorce."

▭ ▭ ▭

Another woman took a little kid to a psychiatrist and said, "Doctor, my boy keeps eating grapes all the time."

The psychiatrist asked, "What's wrong with that?"

"Off the wallpaper!"

My wife is probably the world's worst cook. She has a certain knack of preparing food that's inedible. She cooks from a recipe book called *Condemned by Duncan Hines*.

—   —   —

You should taste some of the dishes she prepares. Did you ever eat baked water?—French fried mustard?—pickled fortune cookies?

—   —   —

Last year she made me a birthday cake with the candles on the inside! Lit!

—   —   —

But I'm just kidding. I love my wife. In fact, I just bought her a present—a new set of stationery, a ball-point pen, and a pound of butter. Every time I go out of town she writes me a greasy love letter.

—   —   —

In my house I don't need any long-playing records, not with *my* wife around.

—   —   —

The good Lord played me a dirty trick. Instead of a tongue he gave her a permanent needle.

▭ ▭ ▭

Nothing confuses a man more than driving behind a woman who does everything right.

▭ ▭ ▭

Take my wife—please!

▭ ▭ ▭

My mother-in-law is not with us. She's in the Congo teaching them to fight dirty.

▭ ▭ ▭

How do you like this new tuxedo—$300. You don't believe it? I'll show you the summons.

▭ ▭ ▭

When you're down and out, lift up your head and shout, "Help!"

▭ ▭ ▭

I want to send my brother-in-law a gift. How do you wrap up a saloon?

□ □ □

A woman is taking a shower. All of a sudden her doorbell rings. She yells, "Who's there?"

He says, "Blind man."

Well, she's a charitable lady. She runs out of the shower naked and opens the door.

He says, "Where should I put these blinds, lady?"

□ □ □

I want to tell you, I have lived. You should have been here Tuesday night. Somebody should have been here. I don't want to say business was bad, but the doorman got locked up for loitering.

□ □ □

Liz Taylor! Take away her long black hair and what have you got? The sexiest bald-headed woman in the world!

□ □ □

I forgot your first *and* your last name.

□ □ □

My wife always complains about something. She always complains about the housework. So I went out and bought her an electric iron, an electric dishwasher, and an electric dryer. She complained—too many gadgets. She had no place to sit down. What do I do to make her happy? I went out and bought her an electric chair.

▭ ▭ ▭

Every place is so jammed nowadays. To get to the other side of the street you have to be born there.

▭ ▭ ▭

Hear about the gypsy who doesn't read the tea leaves? She reads the lemon.

▭ ▭ ▭

I just heard from Bill Bailey. He's not coming home.

▭ ▭ ▭

I just got my TV set insured. If it breaks down they send me a pair of binoculars so I can watch my neighbor's set.

▭ ▭ ▭

But I respect women drivers. I always give them half of the road, when I can figure out which half they want.

▭ ▭ ▭

There's a new device on cars to protect you against teen-age drivers. When you see a teen-ager coming, you press a button. The car folds into the glove compartment till the kid goes by.

▭ ▭ ▭

Would you believe it, I used to play at Carnegie Hall —till the cops chased me away.

▭ ▭ ▭

I feel great. I paid my income tax this month. If anybody has a piece of crayon, please color me broke.

▭ ▭ ▭

At the rate the Kennedys are going, the Republicans won't have a chance. I understand all the Kennedy kids held a meeting up at Hyannis Port last week and decided to apply for statehood.

▭ ▭ ▭

Speaking of taxes, everybody is worried about en tainment expenses. The government wants you to keep diary. I went out with some people the other night. marked everything down—fifty dollars for food, thirty dollars for champagne, ten dollars for tips. The government disallowed it. They found out I was a guest.

I know of one guy who was called in by the tax department and showed up with 400 little black diaries all filled with expenses.

They asked, "What business are you in?"

"I sell little black diaries."

The whole thing is ridiculous. You take somebody to lunch, you can't write it off unless you talk business. I took a blonde to lunch the other day. I started to talk business, she slapped me right in the face.

Just imagine a hot phone between Russia and the United States. If someone accidentally pushes the wrong button, the operator will cut in and say, "Sorry, you have just reached a disconnected nation."

f course the Republicans are worried about the ex-
se. They sent a note to Jack Kennedy saying: "If
u have to use the hot phone, do it after 9:00 o'clock
t night. The rates are cheaper."

━ ━ ━

I hate to take my wife to the movies. She lives the
part of every picture she sees. I took her to see *Days of
Wine and Roses*. She went home and forced herself to
get drunk. I took her to see *The Music Man.* For six
months she took trombone lessons. Next week I'm taking
her to see a picture she won't have any trouble with—
The Ugly American.

━ ━ ━

Everybody is trying to cooperate with President Kennedy's physical fitness program. I know a wealthy guy in
Texas who did not have the time to go on a fifty-mile
hike, so he sent his butler.

━ ━ ━

My wife is crazy about furs and she wanted something
different. So she went to a furrier who does his own
breeding. He crossed a mink with a gorilla. She got a
beautiful coat, only the sleeves are too long.

━ ━ ━

I've been getting a lot of fan mail lately asking me how I can play the violin so badly. I'll let you all in on a secret—the answer is wet resin.

▭ ▭ ▭

Do you know that Jack Benny and I took lessons from the same teacher? *Nero*.

▭ ▭ ▭

In conclusion I leave you with the words of a famous pro football player, who said: "It's not the way you play the game, it's the way you *bet* that counts."

▭ ▭ ▭

Before I go, I have a message for all you parents. Is your teen-age son or daughter out for the evening? If so, take advantage of the opportunity. Pack your furniture, call a moving van, and don't leave a forwarding address.